FUTURE OF THE HOMELAND SECURITY MISSIONS OF THE COAST GUARD

HEARING

BEFORE THE

SUBCOMMITTEE ON BORDER AND MARITIME SECURITY

OF THE

COMMITTEE ON HOMELAND SECURITY HOUSE OF REPRESENTATIVES

ONE HUNDRED THIRTEENTH CONGRESS

SECOND SESSION

FEBRUARY 4, 2014

Serial No. 113–49

Printed for the use of the Committee on Homeland Security

Available via the World Wide Web: http://www.gpo.gov/fdsys/

U.S. GOVERNMENT PRINTING OFFICE

88–023 PDF   WASHINGTON : 2014

For sale by the Superintendent of Documents, U.S. Government Printing Office
Internet: bookstore.gpo.gov   Phone: toll free (866) 512–1800; DC area (202) 512–1800
Fax: (202) 512–2250   Mail: Stop SSOP, Washington, DC 20402–0001

COMMITTEE ON HOMELAND SECURITY

MICHAEL T. MCCAUL, Texas, *Chairman*

LAMAR SMITH, Texas
PETER T. KING, New York
MIKE ROGERS, Alabama
PAUL C. BROUN, Georgia
CANDICE S. MILLER, Michigan, *Vice Chair*
PATRICK MEEHAN, Pennsylvania
JEFF DUNCAN, South Carolina
TOM MARINO, Pennsylvania
JASON CHAFFETZ, Utah
STEVEN M. PALAZZO, Mississippi
LOU BARLETTA, Pennsylvania
RICHARD HUDSON, North Carolina
STEVE DAINES, Montana
SUSAN W. BROOKS, Indiana
SCOTT PERRY, Pennsylvania
MARK SANFORD, South Carolina
VACANCY

BENNIE G. THOMPSON, Mississippi
LORETTA SANCHEZ, California
SHEILA JACKSON LEE, Texas
YVETTE D. CLARKE, New York
BRIAN HIGGINS, New York
CEDRIC L. RICHMOND, Louisiana
WILLIAM R. KEATING, Massachusetts
RON BARBER, Arizona
DONDALD M. PAYNE, JR., New Jersey
BETO O'ROURKE, Texas
TULSI GABBARD, Hawaii
FILEMON VELA, Texas
STEVEN A. HORSFORD, Nevada
ERIC SWALWELL, California

VACANCY, *Staff Director*
MICHAEL GEFFROY, *Deputy Staff Director/Chief Counsel*
MICHAEL S. TWINCHEK, *Chief Clerk*
I. LANIER AVANT, *Minority Staff Director*

————

SUBCOMMITTEE ON BORDER AND MARITIME SECURITY

CANDICE S. MILLER, Michigan, *Chairwoman*

JEFF DUNCAN, South Carolina
TOM MARINO, Pennsylvania
STEVEN M. PALAZZO, Mississippi
LOU BARLETTA, Pennsylvania
VACANCY
MICHAEL T. MCCAUL, Texas *(Ex Officio)*

SHEILA JACKSON LEE, Texas
LORETTA SANCHEZ, California
BETO O'ROURKE, Texas
TULSI GABBARD, Hawaii
BENNIE G. THOMPSON, Mississippi *(Ex Officio)*

PAUL L. ANSTINE, II, *Subcommittee Staff Director*
DEBORAH JORDAN, *Subcommittee Clerk*
ALISON NORTHROP, *Minority Subcommittee Staff Director*

(II)

CONTENTS

FUTURE OF THE HOMELAND SECURITY MISSIONS OF THE COAST GUARD

Tuesday, February 4, 2014

U.S. HOUSE OF REPRESENTATIVES,
SUBCOMMITTEE ON BORDER AND MARITIME SECURITY,
COMMITTEE ON HOMELAND SECURITY,
Washington, DC.

The subcommittee met, pursuant to call, at 10:08 a.m., in Room 311, Cannon House Office Building, Hon. Candice S. Miller [Chairwoman of the subcommittee] presiding.

Present: Representatives Miller, Palazzo, Jackson Lee, Sanchez, O'Rourke, and Gabbard.

Mrs. MILLER. Good morning. The Committee on Homeland Security, Subcommittee on Border and Maritime Security will come to order.

The subcommittee is meeting today to examine the future of the Coast Guard's Homeland Security missions, and our witness today is Admiral Robert Papp, who is the Commandant of the United States Coast Guard. We certainly welcome him.

I am going to recognize myself for an opening statement and then I will give a more formal introduction of Admiral Papp.

Being a life-long recreational boater, I have certainly a deep affinity for the Coast Guard and for the incredible work that they do each and every day, whether it is out on the oceans or in the Great Lakes, whether it is routine boating safety missions, search and rescue, or certainly keeping vital shipping lanes clear of ice in the winter and then helping commerce to flow through all of our channels. I often say that if it is cold and wet and impossible, you should send in the Coast Guard. So we are very appreciative, certainly, of the work that the Coast Guard does in service to our great Nation.

Since 9/11, the Coast Guard has taken an ever-increasing role in the protection of our Nation. We have given the Coast Guard additional responsibilities. We have tasked them to specifically focus their limited resources on port and maritime security. This often calls for some difficult choices, and in this time of very restrained budgets, we have to prioritize the Coast Guard's core missions, because the Coast Guard cannot be everywhere at once.

When the Commandant was before this subcommittee in the last Congress, he stressed the importance of recapitalizing our aging cutter fleet, specifically how important the acquisition of the National Security Cutter was and is. Congress responded, we worked together, and it is on track now to fully fund all eight of the re-

(1)

quired cutters, which I think certainly is vital to the homeland security missions of the Coast Guard.

Again, the Commandant was a very vocal advocate for that, and I am glad that Congress listened to the men and women of the Coast Guard about that issue. However, as we all know, recapitalization of the fleet is long-term, it is a costly process, and in a time again of budget constraints, we have to balance the cost to acquire these advanced cutters against long-term capability needs.

I certainly support the Coast Guard's plan to develop the Offshore Patrol Cutter, or the OPC as it is called, because our older cutters are costing us far too much in terms of less mission readiness, lost operational hours, and higher maintenance costs. Just consider for a moment that major Coast Guard law enforcement cutters have an average age of more than 40 years, while at the same time our naval ships have an average age of only 14. Quite a discrepancy there.

We in the Congress need to ensure that the Coast Guard, again, has the proper assets to safely and effectively carry out its operations. This committee is especially interested in hearing the Commandant's thoughts on the trade-offs required to ensure that the Coast Guard has the capabilities required to secure the maritime borders, to combat terrorism, to interdict drugs, and to perform its other statutory missions.

During the 113th Congress, this subcommittee held a series of hearings on what a secure border looks like. As we increase our efforts along the border, other threats have emerged, such as the growing threat from panga boats off the coast of California.

No border security efforts can be complete without a serious examination of our maritime security, and how we measure success there as well, and it will take an "all of the Department of Homeland Security" approach to securing our borders—Northern, Southern, and our maritime borders.

Thankfully, the Coast Guard is adept at partnering with and leveraging other Department of Homeland Security components in the critical maritime domain. Centers like the Operational Integration Center in Detroit continue to be a good model for cooperation amongst the various Federal partners, State and local stakeholders, in addition to our Canadian friends. We certainly welcome and appreciate the contributions made by the Coast Guard to this collaboration as well as their leadership role in the Regional Coordinating Mechanism, or RCM, as it is called.

Sharing information helps secure the border, minimizes the duplication of efforts between agencies with overlapping jurisdictions, and keeps the maritime domain open for commerce and recreational boaters. One of the more interesting and valuable programs that leverages our partnerships is the Shiprider program, which we have talked about on this committee many times. We have very closely followed the progress of this integrated law enforcement program since it was first piloted in 2006. We were very pleased to see that the permanent authorization of the Shiprider program, that I actually authored and this committee passed, was included in the 2012 Coast Guard Authorization Act.

As you know, this committee has a long history of strongly supporting the specialized maritime security teams that deploy to provide security and protection in a maritime environment and specialize in counterterrorism tactics and is designed as a first responder to marine terrorist situations.

We are very interested on getting the Commandant's perspective on the future of these programs and what advice he might give to the new Commandant when it comes to Homeland Security missions of the Coast Guard.

So, again, I want to thank the Commandant for appearing before us today. We certainly appreciate your presence here, sir. We look forward to hearing your thoughts on how the Congress can work with the Coast Guard to better assist all of the challenges that you have to secure our Nation's ports and maritime borders.

At this time the Chairwoman now recognizes the Ranking Minority Member of the subcommittee, the gentlelady from Texas, Ms. Jackson Lee, for her statement.

Ms. JACKSON LEE. Let me thank the Chairwoman and thank our witness, Commandant Papp, for his leadership and the leadership that has been given by the United States Coast Guard.

I am prone to the work that the Coast Guard has done over the years, and as a beginning and early member of the Homeland Security Committee, I felt that the Coast Guard was a strategic element of the war on terrorism and the prevention of any further attacks on the homeland, and I continue to emphasize both the civilian and military role that the Coast Guard plays, plays in commerce, but it also plays in the security of the Nation's citizens. For that, I am eternally grateful and agree that the funding necessary for the Coast Guard to carry out its responsibilities should be an important responsibility.

I, too, am glad of the funding of the offshore patrol cutters and realize that even though they may have a life of 40 years-plus, it is not the best to continue to utilize equipment that does not have the state-of-the-art technology, although the Coast Guard has been enormously effective in its efforts with the equipment that it has, and I believe that we should continue to seek full funding for the resources of the personnel of the Coast Guard and of the equipment.

Admiral, let me make note of Polar Star, I believe one of our major assets of the Coast Guard, and know that if you had reached the Australian research ship, as you had been requested to do, and you were on your way to do so before mother nature took hold, all would have been well. So let me thank those who manned that and thank the Coast Guard for being ever-ready in its service.

As Ranking Member of the Subcommittee on Border and Maritime Security and a Member of Congress representing the Port of Houston, again, as I indicate, I am well aware of the value of the Coast Guard to our communities and Nation. In my own backyard, the Coast Guard works to secure the Port of Houston, among other ports, which is imperative as it is the Nation's largest petrochemical complex, supplying over 40 percent of our petrochemical manufacturing capacity.

The Coast Guard also works to facilitate commerce, which is vital to our economy, as the Port of Houston handles nearly 230 million tons of cargo annually, making it the No. 1 U.S. port in foreign water-borne tonnage and generating over 650,000 jobs at its terminals. Without the Coast Guard, this would simply not be possible. Of course, these examples are just one small part of the service by U.S. Coast Guard men and women across 11 statutory missions both here at home and around the world.

Given this committee's jurisdiction, the focus of today's hearing is the Coast Guard's Homeland Security missions, including ports, waterways and coastal security, drug interdiction, migrant interdiction, defense readiness, and law enforcement. I am pleased to have the Commandant of the Coast Guard, Admiral Robert Papp, here to discuss the future of these Homeland Security missions.

Personally, Commandant Papp, I want to thank you for 40 years-plus probably of service and your true commitment to America's goals, visions, security, and your service to your Nation. I know that the men and women of the Coast Guard have benefited from your long years of service, and it is my privilege to simply say thank you.

Indeed, this is a particularly appropriate time for him to be before the committee as he completes his 4 years of service as Commandant in May. It is also a critical time for the Coast Guard, as budget cuts and recapitalization challenges force the Coast Guard to make some tough choices. The Coast Guard has been forced to cut back its hours on water and in the air, contributing to a reduction in mission performance. This is a troubling trend that must be reversed. The Coast Guard already provides the American taxpayers with an excellent return on our investment, and there is only so long we can ask them to continue to do more with less.

Frankly, I believe that we should have a goal, as the Chairwoman has worked unceasingly on issues dealing with assets, that we should have a commitment of full funding of the Coast Guard. I am reminded of my own visuals watching the Coast Guard race up and down the Pacific and in the Caribbean area to track and find drug dealers who have taken to the waterways, and taken to the waterways in very large numbers. Other means of attacks on the United States are able to approach us through the waterways, and the Coast Guard is one of our first lines of defense.

So I am here to hear from the Commandant and to thank him as well, and to commit to working to prepare the Coast Guard for its 21st Century multi-missions that it has. Again, I don't think I miss a time when a Coast Guard is before me to say again, among all the things you have done, and you have done many things, I am very much reminded of the work you did in Hurricane Katrina in saving the lives of those stranded in the terrible aftermath of the hurricane and the breaking of the dam that faced the citizens of New Orleans, many of whom now live in Houston, Texas.

Madam Chairwoman, I do want to acknowledge present Congressman Beto O'Rourke and Captain Gabbard, Congresswoman from Hawaii. Commandant, she is with the Hawaiian Army National Guard, Military Police, and she did two deployments in Iraq, but I take note of her because she was on her 2 weeks of military police training in Fort Leonard Wood, Missouri. So we missed her for a while at this committee, and we welcome her back, having done her requirements to serve the Nation in more ways than here in the United States Congress. So let me thank all of you.

With that, Madam Chairwoman, I yield back.

Mrs. MILLER. I thank the gentlelady very much for her comments, and I certainly join with her in recognizing our colleague from Hawaii to be here and for her service to the country, as you say, in many, many ways. We appreciate that.

I also want to join in and again thank the Commandant for his many, many years of service to the Coast Guard and to our Nation. I know your term as Commandant is coming to an end; is it the end of May or beginning of June?

Admiral PAPP. May 30.

Mrs. MILLER. Yeah. May 30. We certainly are going to miss him on this committee and miss your advocacy for the men and women of the Coast Guard. You certainly have done the service, your uniform, and the country very, very proud.

Admiral Robert Papp began his service as Commandant of the United States Coast Guard in May 2010. The Admiral has served in numerous capacities within the Coast Guard, including the commander of the Coast Guard Atlantic area as well as the commander of the Ninth Coast Guard District, a district that includes the Coast Guard missions on the Great Lakes and the Northern Borders. His full statement will appear in the record.

I would also remind the other Members of the committee that if they have any opening statements, we can include those in the record as well.

At this time the Chairwoman now recognizes the Commandant for 5 minutes; actually for as long as you may consume. Please take your time.

STATEMENT OF ADMIRAL ROBERT J. PAPP, COMMANDANT, U.S. COAST GUARD, U.S. DEPARTMENT OF HOMELAND SECURITY

Admiral PAPP. Thank you, Madam Chairwoman.

Thank you also, Ranking Member Jackson Lee, and to the distinguished Members of the panel. Thank you for having me here today.

It has just been an honor to serve in this service that I love so much for nearly 4 decades, but it is an even greater honor to come up here each time to talk about the men and women of the Coast Guard and to try to provide for the resources that they need to get their jobs done, and I am particularly mindful of those men and women today.

I have attended three memorial services this past week as the keynote speaker. Each one of them drove home to me once again the dangerous work that we do and the selfless dedication of the people who do it.

Now, the first two were in Florida and they go back a ways, but we continue to remember our shipmates of the Coast Guard Cutter Blackthorn, which sank 34 years ago in Tampa Bay with the loss of 23 Coast Guardsmen. The third service was out in California, and it was a memorial service for Boatswain's Mate Third Class, Travis Obendorf of the National Security Cutter *Waesche*. He was mortally wounded during a rescue operation in the Bering Sea, and then just around Christmastime, he succumbed to his injuries.

Both these events were fresh reminders to me that downstream from every decision, every hearing, every piece of policy that we produce here in Washington, it is young men and women who carry those things out, often when they are cold, wet, and tired, and who stand the watch to keep our homeland safe.

So I am here today to discuss the Coast Guard's homeland security missions, but before I begin, I would like to thank the Members of the subcommittee for their support in passing the Consolidated Appropriations Act of 2014. This act will really help to relieve the erosive efforts of sequestration on our service. It will also restore front-line operations and badly-needed training hours for my people and ease many of the personnel management restrictions that we had to face over the past year.

I would also like to take this opportunity to thank our new Secretary. Secretary Jeh Johnson has been a tremendously enthusiastic supporter of the Coast Guard in his short time in the Department. I deeply appreciate his concern for our people and also his strong advocacy for our service's critical recapitalization needs.

America is a maritime Nation, we all understand that, and we rely upon the safe, secure, and free flow of goods across the seas into our ports and waterways. I have always firmly believed as a Coast Guardsman that one measure of our Nation's greatness is its ability to provide safe and secure approaches to our ports. This system of uninterrupted trade is the lifeblood of our economy. For more than 2 centuries, the Coast Guard has safeguarded America's maritime interests and kept those approaches secure.

As the Nation's maritime first responder, we protect those on the sea, we protect the Nation from threats delivered by the sea, and we also protect the sea itself. Every day the Coast Guard acts to both prevent and respond to an array of threats that if left unchecked would impede trade, weaken our economy, and create instability. These threats disrupt regional and global security, the economies of our partner nations, and access to both resources and international trade. All of these are vital elements of our National prosperity, which of course plays into our National security.

In previous testimony, I have used the term "layered security" to describe the way the Coast Guard counters maritime threats facing the United States. This layered security strategy first begins in foreign ports, then it spans the high seas, because the best place to counter a threat is before it reaches our borders.

It then encompasses our exclusive economic zone in territorial seas, which is the largest exclusive economic zone in the world at 4.5 million square miles, the largest of any country, and then it continues into our ports and our inland waters.

Now, starting overseas, our international port security program assesses foreign ports on security and anti-terrorism measures. Since the inception of the program in 2004, Coast Guard personnel have visited more than 150 countries and 1,300 port facilities. Vessels sailing from ports where effective counterterrorism measures are not in place force conditions of entry prior to entering our ports or we subject them to additional security measures and inspections before they arrive in our ports.

Our Nation faces a range of risks and vulnerabilities that continue to grow and evolve. The global economy is spurring investment in even larger vessels to ship goods across the seas, and the Arctic is seeing exponential increases in vessel traffic and human activity and we continue to see persistent efforts by terrorists and transnational criminal networks to exploit the maritime environment.

It is Coast Guard's responsibility to detect and interdict contraband and illegal drug traffic, enforce U.S. immigration laws, protect our valuable natural resources and counter threats to U.S. maritime and economic security worldwide, and it is often the most effective to do this as far as possible from our shores.

A capable offshore fleet of cutters is critical to the layered approach, and this is the same area that has caused me concern, as I have mentioned in the past. I am deeply grateful that now we have 8 National Security Cutters in sight, but now we need to move on to our next large project, which is replacing our medium-endurance cutters which, as mentioned, they are averaging 46 years old. In fact, the oldest one turns 50 this year.

I sailed on one of those cutters, the Coast Guard Cutter *Valiant,* when I was a brand-new cadet. The ship was only 3 years old at the time, and *Valiant* has been sailing the better part—by the time I was commissioned in the service, it had been sailing for about a decade. Solely due to the determination of our sailors, our cuttermen, our naval engineers and our modernized mission support system, *Valiant* will still be sailing when I leave the service after nearly 44 years.

So as good as our people are and our support systems are, it is no longer possible to sustain these vessels. In fact, 3 of these same cutters, sister ships, needed emergency dry docks for repairs to their failing hulls this year.

Now, I am fully aware of the fiscal constraints we face as a Nation, but we must continue to support the development of the Offshore Patrol Cutter. I am committed to working with the Department, the administration, and the Congress to ensure we can achieve the Coast Guard's critical recapitalization needs in an affordable manner.

Closer to home, we work with the interagency, the intergovernmental and commercial partners to patrol maritime approaches, escort vessels, monitor critical infrastructure, and inspect port facilities. These partnerships continue to enhance our capability and effectiveness along our coasts and waterways.

To maximize the effectiveness of our efforts, we are a member of the National intelligence community. We screen ships, crews, and passengers bound for the States before they reach our ports. Using our maritime intelligence fusion centers and intelligence coordination center, we work hand-in-hand with Customs and Border Protection to analyze arriving vessels and highlight potential threats. Last year we collectively screened more than 126,000 vessels and over 30 million people seeking to enter the United States. These efforts enhance maritime domain awareness, a key element that supports the Department of Homeland Security layered security strategy.

As the Nation's maritime governance force, the Coast Guard possesses unique authorities, capabilities, and partnerships. Coupled with capable ships, aircraft, and boats operated by highly proficient personnel, we maximize these authorities and capabilities to execute layered security throughout the entire maritime domain, and our many partnerships facilitate the integration of Federal resources with State and local capabilities.

We are a ready force on a continuous watch with a proven ability to surge assets and our people to crisis events when and where they occur.

So I thank you for this opportunity to testify today and I look forward to answering your questions.

[The prepared statement of Admiral Papp follows:]

PREPARED STATEMENT OF ROBERT J. PAPP

FEBRUARY 4, 2014

INTRODUCTION

Good morning, Chairwoman Miller, Ranking Member Jackson Lee, and distinguished Members of the subcommittee. It is a pleasure to be here today to discuss the Coast Guard's homeland security missions.

For more than 2 centuries, the U.S. Coast Guard has safeguarded the Nation's maritime interests on our rivers and ports, in coastal regions, on the high seas, and around the world. The Coast Guard is at all times an armed service, a Federal law enforcement agency, a humanitarian service, and a member of the intelligence community charged with significant safety, security, and stewardship responsibilities in the maritime domain. Every day the Coast Guard conducts search and rescue, escorts vessels carrying dangerous cargoes, interdicts drug and migrant smugglers, patrols our ports and waterways, enforces fisheries laws, responds to oil and hazardous material spills, maintains aids to navigation, screens commercial ships and crews entering U.S. ports, inspects U.S. flagged vessels, examines cargo containers, investigates marine accidents, trains international partners, and supports Overseas Contingency Operations. This diverse mission set and authorities are vital to the safety and security of our Nation's maritime transportation system and essential to our Nation's economic growth. With 223 years of experience as the Nation's maritime first responder, the Coast Guard provides tremendous value and service to the public.

A LAYERED SYSTEM TO COUNTER MARITIME RISK

As a maritime nation, the United States relies on the safe, secure, and free flow of legitimate global commerce on the high seas, throughout the Exclusive Economic Zone (EEZ)—the largest of any country in the world—and inside America's ports and waterways.

With more than 4.5 million square miles of territorial seas and EEZ, 95,000 miles of coastline, 12,000 miles of navigable waters, over 350 ports, and significant international maritime border interests with Canada and Mexico, the U.S. maritime domain is broad in its scope and diversity, requiring an integrated and layered system for security.

The strategy of the Department of Homeland Security (DHS) and the Coast Guard is to increase maritime security through a layered system that reaches beyond the country's physical borders. This system begins in foreign ports, spans the high seas, encompasses the U.S. EEZ and territorial seas, and continues into our ports. The Coast Guard's mix of cutters, aircraft, boats, and deployable specialized forces (DSF), as well as international and domestic partnerships, allow the Coast Guard to leverage its unique maritime security authorities and competencies to reduce risk and improve security throughout the maritime domain.

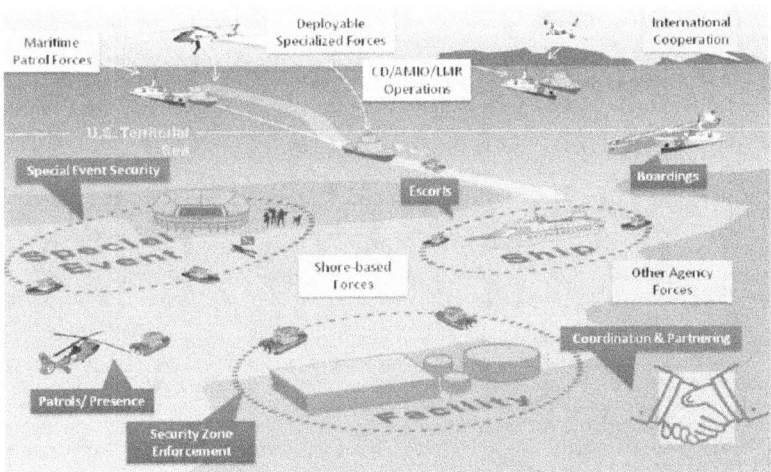

Maritime Domain Awareness (MDA) is one of the most important aspects of the Coast Guard's layered security system and it supports all levels (strategic, operational, and tactical) of decision making. Effective MDA requires efficient information sharing and coordination among numerous participants at international, Federal, regional, State, local, territorial, and Tribal levels of government, as well as with maritime industry and private-sector partners. MDA is more than an awareness of ships en route to a particular port; it also entails knowledge of:

- *People.*—Crew, passengers, owners, and operators;
- *Cargo.*—All elements of the global supply chain;
- *Infrastructure.*—Vital elements of the Nation's maritime infrastructure, including facilities, services, and systems;
- *Environment.*—Weather, environmentally-sensitive areas, and living marine resources;
- *Trends.*—Shipping routes, migration routes, and seasonal changes; and
- *Threats.*—Potential or indication of illicit or hostile activity in the maritime environment.

INTERNATIONAL COOPERATION

Layered security begins overseas. The Coast Guard fosters strategic relationships with partner nations to detect, deter, and counter threats as early and as far from U.S. shores as possible. To achieve that end, the Coast Guard conducts foreign port assessments and leverages the International Maritime Organization's (IMO) International Ship and Port Facility Security (ISPS) Code to assess effectiveness of security and antiterrorism measures in foreign ports. The ISPS Code provides an international regime to ensure ship and port facilities take appropriate preventative measures consistent with our domestic regime under the Maritime Transportation Security Act. Through the International Port Security Program, the Coast Guard performs overseas port assessments to determine the effectiveness of security and antiterrorism measures exhibited by foreign trading partners. Since the inception of the International Port Security Program in 2004, Coast Guard personnel have visited more than 150 countries and approximately 1,300 port facilities. These countries generally receive biennial assessments to verify compliance with the ISPS Code and U.S. maritime security regulations. Vessels arriving in non-ISPS Code-compliant countries are required to take additional security precautions while in those ports and may subject to boarding and inspection by the Coast Guard before being granted permission to enter U.S. ports. In specific cases, these vessels may be refused entry. Furthermore, the International Port Security Program conducts targeted capacity building efforts to help countries that fail to meet ISPS Code achieve compliance, and to prevent countries with marginal compliance from falling into non-compliance.

SECURITY AND GOVERNANCE ON THE HIGH SEAS

America's diplomatic strength and economic security depend upon the free flow of global commerce and a proper system of governance in the maritime domain. Coast Guard responsibilities on the high seas include detecting and interdicting contraband and illegal drug traffic, enforcing U.S. immigration laws at sea, and countering threats to maritime and economic security worldwide. A capable fleet of Maritime Patrol Forces (comprised of Coast Guard cutters and aircraft, and their crews) and DSF are critical to the layered security approach.

Within the EEZ, the Coast Guard enforces our Nation's living marine resources (LMR) and marine-protected species laws and regulations to ensure the integrity of the EEZ, and to ensure the continued viability of critical fish stocks. This enforcement involves the deterrence, detection, and interdiction of illegal incursions into the EEZ by foreign fishing vessels. As these incursions represent a threat to our Nation's renewable natural resources and sovereignty, the protection of the United States EEZ contributes to another fundamental layer of the Coast Guard maritime security system.

Coast Guard at-sea presence ensures compliance with international agreements for the management of LMR through enforcement of conservation and management measures created by Regional Fishery Management Organizations (RFMOs). Of the 4.5 million square miles that comprise the EEZ, more than 75% is outside the contiguous zone of the United States.

The Coast Guard maintains a strong at-sea presence to disrupt the maritime flow of illegal drugs and other contraband through the maritime drug transit zone. This presence supports National and international strategies to deter and disrupt the market for illegal drugs, dismantle Transnational Organized Crime (TOC) networks, and prevent transnational threats from reaching the United States. Through 45 established bilateral agreements, the Coast Guard facilitates coordination of operations and the forward deployment of boats, cutters, aircraft, and personnel to deter and counter threats as close to their origin as possible. By extending our law enforcement capabilities into the territorial seas of other countries, the Coast Guard is at the forefront in assisting partner nations' efforts to reduce the production and transportation of illicit drugs within their sovereign boundaries.

The Coast Guard also relies on joint, interagency, and international partnerships to conduct drug interdiction. More specifically, the Coast Guard leverages the availability of U.S. Navy and Allied Nation vessels to enhance presence and expand interdiction opportunities by embarking specially-trained Law Enforcement Detachments (LEDET). Coast Guard LEDETs employ their distinctive law enforcement authorities to stop threats and to gather critical information regarding vessels, crew, passengers, and cargo destined for the United States. Over the last 5 years, Coast Guard Maritime Patrol Forces and LEDETs have removed approximately 500 metric tons of cocaine, with a wholesale value of nearly $17 billion.

The Coast Guard enforces U.S. immigration laws and international conventions against human smuggling through at-sea interdiction and rapid repatriation of undocumented migrants attempting to reach the United States unlawfully. The Coast Guard maintains a constant law enforcement presence at-sea to deter undocumented migrants and transnational human smugglers from using maritime routes to enter the United States, to detect and interdict undocumented migrants and smugglers far from the U.S. border, and to expand Coast Guard participation in multi-agency and international border security initiatives. The Coast Guard accomplishes this mission in conjunction with other Federal, State, and local agencies, including U.S. Citizenship and Immigration Services (USCIS), Immigration and Customs Enforcement (ICE), Customs and Border Protection (CBP), and the Department of State. While the Coast Guard leads the interdiction mission on the high seas, partnerships with CBP and ICE are critical for successful shore-side interdiction operations.

The United States is also an Arctic nation, with significant interests in the future of the region. As oil and natural gas exploration in the Arctic attracts significant interest from the international community, the importance of the Arctic is more critical than ever. The Coast Guard, as the maritime component of the U.S. Department of Homeland Security (DHS), has specific statutory responsibilities in U.S. Arctic waters. U.S. Coast Guard continues to assess its responsibilities in support of the emerging economic, environmental, and political issues, and will help advance our interests in that region.

In the rapidly-evolving geopolitical landscape, the United States must maintain an offshore maritime presence to promote Maritime Governance and to protect America's National and homeland security interests. Moreover, with renewed National focus on the Asia Pacific, emerging international interest in the Arctic, and continuing obligations in the Western Hemisphere, a versatile U.S. Coast Guard off-shore capability is an important component of the Coast Guard's layered security strategy.

SECURITY IN COASTAL WATERS

To address potential threats approaching our shores, Coast Guard ships, boats, aircraft, and DSF provide the ability to monitor, track, interdict, and board vessels. In addition, interagency partnerships have an increasing role in the layered security approach. Coast Guard Area Commanders receive support from the National Vessel Movement Center and Maritime Intelligence Fusion Centers (MIFCs), which screen commercial vessels operating within their areas of responsibility. The MIFCs focus on screening characteristics associated with the vessels itself, such as ownership, ownership associations, cargo, and previous activity. Coast Guard vessel screening results are disseminated to the appropriate DHS Maritime Interagency Operations Center (IOC), Sector Command Center, local intelligence staffs, CBP, and other interagency partners to evaluate and take action on any potential risks. Additionally, vessel screening develops a manageable set of targets for potential Coast Guard boardings and/or inspections by Maritime Patrol Forces, Shore-Based Forces, or DSF. Complementary screening efforts occur at the National and tactical levels. At the National level, the Intelligence Coordination Center's Coastwatch Branch, which is co-located with CBP at the National Targeting Center, screens crew and passenger information. Through our partnership with CBP, we have expanded access to counterterrorism, law enforcement, and immigration databases, and this integration has led to greater information sharing and more effective security operations. In 2013, Coastwatch screened approximately 126,000 Advance Notice of Arrivals (ANOAs) and 30.7 million crew and passenger records of vessels before they entered U.S. Ports.

SECURITY IN U.S. PORTS AND INTERAGENCY PARTNERSHIPS

In the Nation's 361 maritime ports, the Coast Guard, along with our Federal, State, local, and Tribal partners, working in concert with port stakeholders, patrol our waters and critical infrastructure, conduct vessel escorts, and inspect vessels and facilities. The Coast Guard utilizes data from its Maritime Security Risk Analysis Model (MSRAM) for prioritizing security escorts and patrols. MSRAM is a terrorism risk analysis tool and methodology used at all Coast Guard Sectors to perform detailed risk analysis of the Marine Transportation System (MTS), maritime Critical Infrastructure, and other potential targets, such as large congregations of people in the maritime domain. MSRAM offers an analytical interface capable of generating tailored results to support risk-based decision making at the strategic, operational, and tactical levels.

Coast Guard Captains of the Port (COTPs), in their role as Federal Maritime Security Coordinator (FMSC), significantly enhance domestic maritime transportation security and preparedness through long-standing cooperation and coordination with their respective Area Maritime Security Committees.

As the FMSC, the Coast Guard COTP works in partnership with Government and private-sector AMSC members to manage the Nation's 43 Area Maritime Security (AMS) Plans. These plans provide Government and private industry port partners with a coordination and communication framework to prevent, protect against, respond to, and recover from a Transportation Security Incident or the threat thereof. The COTPs and their respective AMSCs validate their AMS Plan and ensure plan familiarity by conducting annual exercises, as required by the Maritime Transportation Security Act (MTSA). In and around our ports, the Coast Guard also maintains robust multi-mission maritime first responder assets capable of saving lives, protecting property and the environment, and responding to disasters within the maritime domain. The Coast Guard leverages its broad COTP authorities and its role as FMSC and Federal On-Scene Coordinator to coordinate response to disasters such as BP Deepwater Horizon and Hurricane Sandy. The Coast Guard is also working with other components of DHS and with the maritime sector to determine how the critical infrastructure security and resilience guidance of Executive Order 13636 and Presidential Policy Directive 21 should be leveraged by the community.

Coast Guard Maritime Security and Response Operations (MSRO) apply our authorities, competencies, capabilities, capacities, and partnerships to deny the use and exploitation of the maritime domain by criminal or hostile actors. The Coast Guard coordinates the activities of many Federal, regional, State, Tribal, territorial, and local Government agencies as well as the maritime industry to prevent, disrupt, protect, respond to, and recover from terror-related risks in the maritime domain. In 2013, Coast Guard forces conducted:

- More than 670 security boardings of high-interest vessels;
- Close to 8,500 security boardings of small vessels;
- More than 2,000 escorts of high-capacity passenger vessels, e.g., ferries and cruise ships;
- More than 1,200 escorts of high-value U.S. naval vessels transiting U.S. waterways; and
- More than 690 escorts of vessels carrying certain dangerous cargoes.

Maritime Security Response Operations enhance the resilience of maritime CIKR and the MTS. As such, MSRO plays a critical role in the Coast Guard's Ports, Waterways, and Coastal Security mission by deterring adversaries, maximizing the probability of disrupting their pre-operational planning, and providing a response framework to prevent and respond to maritime transportation security incidents.

MARITIME THREAT RESPONSE

When the Coast Guard is alerted to a specific maritime security threat to the United States that requires a coordinated U.S. Government response, the Maritime Operational Threat Response (MOTR) Plan is activated. The MOTR Plan uses established protocols and an integrated network of National-level maritime command and operations centers to facilitate real-time Federal interagency communication, coordination, and decision making to ensure a timely, unified, and decisive response to maritime threats.

Coast Guard DSF are highly-trained, proficient forces that provide field commanders with the ability to rapidly respond to emerging threats throughout the maritime environment, including threats of terrorism and weapons of mass destruction. The Coast Guard has also established a Chemical, Biological, Radiological, Nuclear, and Explosives (CBRNE) program and has worked extensively with DHS's Domestic Nuclear Detection Office and U.S. Special Operations Command to train and equip Coast Guard personnel to detect and respond to CBRNE threats in the maritime domain.

CONCLUSION

The Coast Guard's layered security regime is vital to the Nation's security. Our authorities, capabilities, competencies, and partnerships provide the President, Secretary of Homeland Security, Secretary of Defense, and other National leaders with a ready force and the capabilities to lead or support a range of operations to ensure safety, security, and stewardship in the maritime domain. Through this interconnected system, the Coast Guard stands ready to meet offshore, coastal, and port threats that have the potential to impact our National security and economic prosperity. From our efforts to improve maritime domain awareness to our international and domestic partnerships, and investments in cutter, boat, and aircraft recapitalization, the Coast Guard continues to improve the maritime security system to counter maritime threats and facilitate the safe flow of legitimate commerce.

Thank you for the opportunity to testify today, and thank you for your continued support of the U.S. Coast Guard. I would be pleased to answer your questions.

Mrs. MILLER. Thank you very much, Admiral.

As I mentioned to you before we began this hearing, coming from the Detroit sector, State of Michigan, from the Great Lakes region, I have to start off with a question about your icebreaking capabilities in the Great Lakes. We, as everybody knows, had a really particularly cold, frigid winter. I heard the other day that there is more ice cover on Lake Superior than has ever been recorded before. I am not sure if that is true, but certainly when you look at some of these aerials, there is as much ice as I can ever remember seeing.

With the very bitter cold that happened, we have got—when that ice starts melting here in the spring, we are going to have some tremendous ice jams happening through some of the areas of the Great Lakes, through the St. Claire River, all these navigable waterways that make up our commerce shipping lanes. Obviously, maritime shipping commerce in the Great Lakes is a multi-billion dollar industry, so very, very critical.

I am just wondering, in fact, I have had an opportunity in past years of going out to accompanying on a mission for some icebreaking. It is interesting to watch that happen. I think next week I am going to be doing the same kind of a thing up in the Great Lakes basin, again just on a dedicated mission that you were already going on to be able to sort of observe some of those things, but I also was looking at the list of the icebreaking capability that you have in the Great Lakes, and it is a remarkable inventory, although probably never enough.

So I guess I would just ask you first to comment a bit on your current resources that you have, because, as I say, I think this spring, we have the potential of having probably some of the biggest ice jams that have ever happened there, and so, sir, if you could a little bit, how would you sort-of try to keep ahead of that with the resources that you have? Do you have to move the icebreaking capability around the Great Lakes basin a bit?

I know you are in the process of refurbishing some of your icebreakers there. Then are you, as far as authorizing additional, what is your thought on current and then going into the future there?

Admiral PAPP. Madam Chairwoman, as you know, the Great Lakes are near and dear to my heart as a previous commander up there. I think even back now 4, 6, 8, almost 10 years ago when I went up there as the commander, one of the things I recognized was the 140-foot icebreakers were getting old, they were well past their mid-age, and we had not done any renovations on them.

One of the things I was really proud of was that as the district commander, I put in a request to move an additional icebreaker up there. When I moved to be the area commander, I endorsed it and sent it on to Coast Guard headquarters. By the time I became Commandant, it got to my desk and I approved the extra icebreaker for the Great Lakes.

Actually, it was good that we did that at the time. It was because they were becoming increasingly unreliable due to maintenance issues and age.

I am very happy to report this year that we now have a program in place, it is called the in-service vessel sustainment project. In fact, *Morro Bay,* from Cleveland, will be the first ship to go into that. We estimate it is going to cost about $14 million per ship. The first one, *Morro Bay,* will take about 12 months as the Coast Guard yard goes through the process and learns lessons from it, and then we will subsequently put each one of the 140's through there and it will take each one about 9 months.

So there will be at times when we will go from 6 down to 5 up on the Great Lakes as we go through this process, but the end result is going to be more reliable icebreakers up there. *Mackinaw,* of course, is relatively new in Coast Guard terms, and the 2 225 buoy tender icebreakers are relatively new in Coast Guard terms as well.

So I am very pleased with what we have up there. This winter's an anomaly. It will really test our resources, but I think we are well-prepared for it.

The other thing that I would add is that the Coast Guard reaches out internationally. We meet annually with the Canadian

Coast Guard. The commissioner and I hold a summit meeting, and part of what we do is work with our Canadian partners who have icebreakers as well. We have a command center that stands up every winter there so that we can balance both Canadian and U.S. needs. Oftentimes we are breaking in Canadians and Canadian vessels are breaking paths for us, and we get the best out of the resources of our two countries to keep the lakes open.

Mrs. MILLER. I appreciate that, Admiral. Just another issue there, I suppose, as we have talked about the water assets that you have now in regards to the air assets that you have, it is my understanding with the types of helicopters that you have, to the Great Lakes basin again, that there is very limited amount, if any, of helicopters that have de-icing capability.

Admiral PAPP. Right.

Mrs. MILLER. If that is the case, it just strikes you as very odd. Obviously it limits your ability, I would think, depending on the weather conditions, if you don't have de-icing capability. What can we do to assist with the—first of all, is that true, there is no de-icing, and second, what could this committee do to assist to make sure that people are resourced properly there as well?

Admiral PAPP. Right. Yes, ma'am. Our short-range recovery helicopters, the H–65s, both Air Station Traverse City and Air Station Detroit, that is their inventory, is H–65s. If you go back in history at Traverse City, there was a time where we had H–3 helicopters, which now have been replaced by the H–60, which is our medium-range helicopter. The bigger the helicopter, the more powerful it is, the more equipment you can put in it; and when they become smaller, you conserve by the amount of equipment that you put in it in order to get endurance. The decision was made a long time ago to put H–65s at both those stations. I was an advocate 10 years ago to put the H–60 helicopter at Traverse City.

It is not just the de-icing. H–60s do have de-icing, and that would come in helpful, but it is also the range that the helicopters have to fly up there. I literally was on a flight leaving from Traverse City to go down to Duluth. We had to stop and refuel before we got to Duluth in an H–65. You generally get about 2 hours of endurance in an H–65. You get about 6 hours of endurance in an H–60, plus greater lift and weather capability.

It is not just to the western extreme in Superior. We also often had to rely upon the Canadians in Lake Ontario because we couldn't get all the way over there from our air stations.

So the H–60 if it was in Traverse City would give us much more capability both in weather and in range, and I think that is a wise operational decision. We have put that forward a number of times, but in order to do that, we would—and move helicopters around, we would need to close down the two air facilities that sit on Lake Michigan and Waukegan and Muskegon as a tradeoff in order to do that, but I think on balance, having the greater capability of the H–60 far outweighs having those two air facs.

Plus, we have put increased surface assets, faster boats, more capable boats around Lake Michigan as well, which mitigates any impact that those air fac closures would have.

Mrs. MILLER. I appreciate those comments, and we certainly will consider them here on this committee, as well as I also sit on the

Transportation and Infrastructure Committee on the Coast Guard Subcommittee there, and when we do the authorization for the Coast Guard, I am going to keep all those comments in mind as well.

Just my last question as well, one of the things that this subcommittee has talked about extensively in the last number of years is how we can really advantage the various agencies as we draw down and return from theater with the types of equipment that we have had in Iraq, Afghanistan, et cetera, and really try to make sure that we get the best bang for the taxpayers' buck on equipment that can be utilized, as I say, by other agencies. I do know that the Air Force gave the Coast Guard, or transferred, I should say, to the Coast Guard recently some C–27s, I think 14 of them?

Admiral PAPP. Yes, ma'am.

Mrs. MILLER. Do you have those now or you are getting them now, and how do you anticipate you would utilize those?

Admiral PAPP. So legislation has been passed for the transfer, and in the fiscal year 2014 budget, we received money to stand up a project office to facilitate the swap. It is tracking nicely. I don't have the exact time line right now, but it will be in short order. We will be transferring all 14 over and start converting them to Coast Guard use.

Mrs. MILLER. Okay. Good. We appreciate that.

The Chairwoman recognizes the gentlelady from Texas.

Ms. JACKSON LEE. Let me again thank the Chairwoman, and thank the Commandant very much.

Let me say that as I pose these questions, I do so for establishing on the record that we have to listen to your counsel and advice. For someone who served for 40 years and spent his time among his men and women in the Coast Guard and seeing what their needs are, I think this should be a telling moment in your testimony as to how we move forward. So let me thank you very much.

I just want to put on the record in confirming some of the statements that you made in your testimony this morning that in its annual review of the United States Coast Guard mission performance, the DHS Office of Inspector General found that the total number of vessel and aircraft resource hours available to conduct Coast Guard missions declined by over 6,600 hours for fiscal year 2012. This decline was due to increased rates of asset failures, the decommission of obsolete assets before new assets are acquired to replace them, and reduced funding available to support operations.

Now, I do agree that the work of the Coast Guard has been unparalleled with respect to keeping these assets going, but I think it is clear that we have to listen, and as the Chairwoman indicated, where we were able to get some new equipment, that we need to continue to build on the importance of restoring the Coast Guard's very important equipment.

So I would like to ask a few questions along those lines, making note of the fact that the Coast Guard has 42,000 active-duty, 8,200 reserve, 8,000 civilian personnel carrying out 11 statutory missions. You in your earlier testimony indicated the importance of making sure the ship remains on course. So let me just ask one question as I lead into more specific questions.

If you could, Commandant, just tell us, where do you think the Coast Guard stands today?

Admiral PAPP. Well, we have some of the best people, first of all. Let me start with the people. Of those 42,000, 8,200 and 8,000 active-duty, reserve and civilians, they are some of the finest people I have seen in my entire career. I recognized a number of people at an all-hands meeting last week.

Three relatively junior enlisted people, all three of them had college degrees, in fact, one of them has a master's degree and others are working on their master's degrees. Our retention is the highest it has ever been. People want to serve. We are having to come up with extraordinary measures to reduce our workforce just to keep a healthy flow going through. So I could not be more pleased with the young men and women, the young Americans that are stepping forward now to serve in the Coast Guard.

Where I perhaps feel I am letting them down from time to time is that I have had a focus on proficiency. One of the things that really concerned me when I became Commandant was we had lost, in a 2-year period, we had lost 14 aviators due to accidents, and we had a number of boat accidents, in fact, one resulted in the death of an 8-year-old child, a civilian, and other associated accidents, but the rate of Coast Guard people dying in operational situations was just deplorable.

So we have restored a focus on proficiency, a focus on mission excellence, but where we start to let those people down, who are intent on becoming the best they can be, is when we get into measures like sequestration where the money has to come out of our operating funds, it comes out of the flight hours, the boat hours, the cutter days underway, where our people gain that proficiency. So we are shortchanging our people to a certain extent, and that has me worried.

That is why the fiscal year 2014 budget as passed is a relief for me, because the effects of sequestration will be long-term, but you get lagging indicators for that in terms of training and proficiency. I didn't want to go back to a time when we weren't focused on proficiency, so restoring these hours through the 2014 budget are going to help us quite a bit.

We have recapitalized almost our entire boat fleet due to the administration and the Congress. Our in-shore portion of the Coast Guard is the best I have ever seen it. We have put more people at our stations, we have deployable specialized forces. We have practically brand-new boats, 500 boats throughout the Coast Guard and they are all practically brand-new.

But having said that, that is very well-defended, the coastal portion and our ports, but in football terms, that is doing red zone defense, that they are inside the 20-yard line when they get to that point in our ports.

So the one area that is really deficient is the offshore portion of our fleet. Those ships that I spoke of that are—we now have the replacements, the National Security Cutter, for our high-endurance cutters that we are retiring.

The next thing is to turn to replacing those medium-endurance cutters that are, as I said, 46 years on average and some now that will be going over 50 years old this year. That is a very expensive proposition, but it is needed, because we can't continue to run the old ships. I also as Commandant need to look out 10, 20, 30, and 40 years from now in terms of what tools will the Coast Guard need then, because they have to be built now.

So people-wise, we are in good shape. Our shore is in relatively good shape, our forces close to shore. It is the off-shore fleet that takes care of that largest exclusive economic zone in the world that we need to pay our attention to.

Ms. JACKSON LEE. So the NSC is fine, but we need to do work on the OPC and the fast response as well?

Admiral PAPP. Well, the NSC is working fine, the 3 that we have out there are great. No. 4 will be out there in October, the *Hamilton,* and we have 6—5, 6, 7, and 8 paid—I am sorry—5, 6, and 7 paid for. We have long lead money for No. 8, and I am hopeful that the construction cost for 8 will be in the 2015 budget.

Ms. JACKSON LEE. Let me give you two quick questions, and I will just say them together, if you don't mind.

Admiral PAPP. Sure.

Ms. JACKSON LEE. Then if you could just—I went to Mumbai soon after the attack in Mumbai, India, and although they were not fancy boats, they were attacks coming off water, and obviously without protection. My interest would be, how equipped are we to prevent terrorist attacks from offshore vessels, water vessels? Some of our beaches and areas are equally unprotected around America.

The other is, too, I have watched the TWIC card, I am a TWIC card holder, I think I may be on an expiration point right now, so I need to get in line, but I have witnessed the implementation and we have discussed it and your members have discussed it. In May 2013, the Government Accountability Office released a report calling into question the current Government-centric approach to port security credentialing, which DHS is responsible, for the enrollment card issuance and security vetting is the best option. Should this Government-centric permits to the TW—to TWIC card be revisited, and what do you think needs to be done? So two questions, on the terrorism ability and this issue dealing with the TWIC card.

Thank you very much.

Admiral PAPP. Yes, ma'am. I would never sit here and tell you that a Mumbai-type attack could not happen in the United States, that would be foolish, but we are doing everything we can to prevent a Mumbai-type attack. Given that we have the broad expanse of the Pacific and the Atlantic, generally we will have warnings, and it would probably have to come from a ship that is offshore if it happened.

Two things on that. First of all, you have to have good intelligence, and that is why it was so important for the Coast Guard to be included in the intelligence community, because we can leverage the Department of Defense and the other intelligence agency partners to keep track of potential threats that are coming towards our shores, learn about them in advance, and interdict them as far off shore as possible.

Once again, validation, justification, why we need an off-shore fleet so we can interdict anything coming towards our shores, so that we can have a persistent presence out there.

If it does get close, we have a robust partnership, we have area maritime security committees that are run by Coast Guard captains of the port in 44 areas of our country that work with Federal, State, and local partners and intelligence community and others to keep track of what is coming into our ports, to screen and vet any potential threats, any ships and passengers that are coming into our ports, and I think that is working well. As I say, we have our conventional forces within the ports, and we are allocating them through risk-based measures to do random patrols to make sure that critical infrastructure is taken care of.

The other aspect that I would like to point out is, that I am proud of is that our deployable specialized forces, the MSST's and the MSRT that were created after 9/11, we got the resources, we put them together, they were overseen by what we call the deployable operations group, but we didn't have strategy, we didn't have doctrine on how we were going to employ them.

One of the things we set to work immediately on is first of all doing a stem-to-stern review of all our deployable specialized forces and how we employ them and then get the doctrine out there. We started with first of all a new publication, Coast Guard Pub 3.0, which describes how we conduct Coast Guard operations, but 3.1 talks about how we integrate deployable specialized forces and why do we need deployable specialized forces.

That is in Pub 3.2: short notice maritime response, advanced interdiction, picking people up before they get into our ports, and that is what we have been training and directing our deployable specialized forces, the maritime safety and security teams, and the maritime security response team to be prepared to take on those challenges.

Ms. JACKSON LEE. Thank you.

Mrs. MILLER. Thank you very much, Admiral.

Ms. JACKSON LEE. Thank you.

Mrs. MILLER. The Chairwoman now recognizes the gentleman from Mississippi, Mr. Palazzo.

Mr. PALAZZO. Thank you, Madam Chairwoman. Admiral Papp.

Admiral PAPP. Good morning, sir.

Mr. PALAZZO. It is a pleasure to see you today. Good morning. Thank you for coming to tell us about your needs and the needs of the men and women in the U.S. Coast Guard.

You mentioned the *Hamilton* briefly. Somebody wants me to say how is your wife, Linda, doing and is she looking forward to the commissioning in the near future?

Admiral PAPP. She is. I didn't mention that my wife is the sponsor for the Coast Guard Cutter *Hamilton*. She smashed the champagne bottle a couple months ago on the ship and will do the commissioning in Charleston probably in October, but I will just be a retired Coast Guardsman at the time, her husband attending with her.

Mr. PALAZZO. Yeah. Well, it is you know, south Mississippi and Huntington Ingalls, we appreciate your trips and visits to the shipyard down there, and it is going to be a fantastic ship, and she should be very proud. It is a state-of-the-art craft.

One of the things you and I have discussed in the past concern the shipbuilding needs of the Coast Guard. We have spoken at length about the NSC and the future of that program, but also about the balancing act that you are required to do with other ships as well, such as the OPC, the icebreaker.

Do you feel like the current budget, you touched on this, is on a better track for meeting your needs and the needs of the Coast Guard since we have last spoken?

Admiral PAPP. Well, sir, I think I have said this before as well, any service chief—no service chief will ever come up here and say, I have got all the money I want, and I don't have all the money I would like. There are many things that I would like to do for my service, but I—as a taxpayer and as a steward of the taxpayers' money, at a certain point in time in the negotiation process—and I do believe that each year I have gotten a fair hearing from my secretaries and OMB and the President.

At a certain point, I am told what my top line is and then I have to juggle and balance and make some compromises, yes, from time to time to make sure that we are taking care of current-day operations but also planning for the future so that those future Coast Guardsmen will have the right tools to work with 10, 20, 30, 40 years from now.

So it has been a balancing act, but we did not think that we were going to get 8 National Security Cutters, and we are on the verge of getting that right now, and we are very close to doing a down select for three candidates to design the Offshore Patrol Cutter, and I am very optimistic about that program. Then we will have to figure out, or my relief will have to figure out how we fit those things in the budget in subsequent years.

Mr. PALAZZO. Do you feel like you have the flexibility to basically meet the needs of your shipbuilding plan?

Admiral PAPP. I——

Mr. PALAZZO. The right mix of ships?

Admiral PAPP. I think so at this point. The administration's been giving me enough to keep our programs going. The Congress has at certain points plussed that up a little bit to help us, for instance, the long lead money that was put in the 2014 budget to—for NSC No. 8, so the process has been working and we have had enough flexibility to keep our programs going on the time line that we predicted.

Mr. PALAZZO. Is there anything that the House can do to ensure that the men and women in the U.S. Coast Guard have the tools and equipment that they need so they can do their jobs, do it safely, and come back home to their families?

Admiral PAPP. Well, I would say that the men and women of the Congress should scrutinize every appropriations bill that comes up here, and you have to make balanced decisions on where the priorities are, listen to people like me who are trying to advocate to make sure that people have the right tools, and then make decisions with good counsel.

Mr. PALAZZO. Well, Admiral, I appreciate that.

I would just like to add a few comments. I mean, it seems like we are continuously fighting over shrinking discretionary funds, you know, the Coast Guard budget, DOD, NASA, pretty much every discretionary agency that falls under that, we continue to fight over it. We understand that, you know, we need this equipment, we need these tools, we need to be able to protect the homeland, but we also need to be able to protect America's interests at home and abroad.

I think, you know, it is unfair to all Americans that we need to get our financial affairs in order, and we have to do that by addressing the No. 1 driver of our deficits and our debt, and that is out-of-control mandatory spending, so that we can continue to fund the U.S. Coast Guard, because not only do the men and women in the Coast Guard deserve it, but Americans expect it.

So sir, I know you are looking forward to your retirement. Enjoy it. Thank you for, you know, not only what your wife's doing sponsoring the NSC *Hamilton,* but good luck in your next endeavors. Thank you.

Admiral PAPP. Well, thank you, sir.

I wouldn't want to leave here with you thinking that I don't appreciate and comprehend the challenges that we find in the budget. As I said earlier, when I am given a top line, that is when I make the tough decisions on what we are going to continue, what we can do, and how we balance current operations versus the future, but along the way, it is not my job to decide what that top line is. My job is to identify the resources we are going to need, what are our requirements.

In my best judgment, based on 40 years, 14 years at sea and doing Coast Guard operations across the full spectrum of what we do, what do we need to do those tools? I don't think there is anybody better-prepared at this juncture than I am, after 4 decades, to say these are the requirements that we have. You may not be able to fund them all, but it is my job to be honest and forthright and candid in terms of what we need, and I have tried to do that every time I have come up here.

Mr. PALAZZO. We appreciate that candor. Thank you.

I yield back.

Admiral PAPP. Yes, sir.

Mrs. MILLER. Thank the gentleman.

The Chairwoman now recognizes the gentleman from Texas, Mr. O'Rourke.

Mr. O'ROURKE. Thank you.

Mr. Commandant, I would also like to join my colleagues in thanking you for your service and through you thanking the men and women who serve our country in the Coast Guard.

Admiral PAPP. Thank you, sir.

Mr. O'ROURKE. I want to follow up on some of the comments you just made in some of the questioning that we have had from the committee today about budgets and some of the tough choices that you have to make in working with that top line number that you keep referring to.

I was reading some comments of yours from a speech that you gave in 2012, and one of the things that you said is that we have to have the courage to be able to say no sometimes, and you talked about decreasing resources, and the Ranking Member talked about fewer than—or we had less than 6,000 hours from previous year this past year in terms of time that we could spend on missions with the Coast Guard, and you have additional responsibilities in the Arctic as more water is freed up and there is more energy exploration there. In your comments in 2012 you were talking about additional responsibilities when it comes to cyber threats and standing up a cyber command within the Coast Guard and adding to what the Department of Defense is already doing.

The way that it was summarized in an article I read, the headline said, "Shrinking Coast Guard Must Cut Drug War to Boost Cyber and Arctic." I wondered—and I know that the nature of headlines is to sensationalize what people say and to draw a reader in, but I wondered if you could reflect a little bit on some of those tough choices, the additional responsibilities and where we might have to say no through the Coast Guard and as a country when it comes to the various threats that we face at our maritime ports and beyond the ports.

Admiral PAPP. Sure.

Going back to what you said originally, one of our greatest strengths in our service culturally is a can-do attitude. One of our greatest weaknesses is a can-do attitude as well, because oftentimes we take on more than we can with the resources that we have, and we get examples like that all the time.

For instance, back about a year or more when we only had one icebreaker, the *Healy,* in service, and it was active in the Arctic, we got a request because a leased, I think it was a leased Finnish or Russian icebreaker that the National Science Foundation had contracted for was not going to be able to go down and break out McMurdo, and they put in a request to take our one icebreaker. It would have been tempting to charge off and put our people through more work and go down there, but I said no, because we only have one icebreaker, the Arctic is our territory, our exclusive economic zone, and I can't take the only icebreaker that the United States had in service and send it down there. It was a tough decision.

We don't have as many large cutters now as we had in the past. We used to be able to participate in Navy exercises throughout the Pacific, and frankly, it is time well spent for our country, because there are countries that want to have coast guards and they enjoy seeing our ships and our sailors, we do cooperative training, but the Arctic has opened up now and we need to send one of our cutters up there, so we had to pull out of Navy exercises, something we hadn't done in decades, in order to provide the ship days to go up and take care of our responsibilities in the Arctic.

So those are the types of things I am talking about. Rather than chase the—I call it, chasing shiny balls, you know, things that are really attractive and we want to race off and do them, we have to stick to the work that we are required to do in a decreased resource environment.

Counter-drug, there is no way we would voluntarily cut back on counter-drug, because it is such a successful program for us. The only reason we cut back this past year, and we had about a 30 percent reduction this year in drugs disrupted, because of sequestration. When you get almost a $200 million bill, which was what sequestration was for the Coast Guard, the only place you can take it out of is discretionary spending, and discretionary spending generally equates to operational hours, whether it is flight hours, boat hours, or ship days, and the only place that we could squeeze it a little bit was in drug interdiction and migrant interdiction.

Mr. O'ROURKE. In terms of measuring the outcomes of those reduced resources and reduced interdictions, are you able to track what that means in terms of availability of those drugs on the streets in the United States or the number of, and I don't know how you'd measure this, but the migrants who are able to get through because of lack of resources? In other words, do we know the outcome, the effect of this?

Admiral PAPP. Yes, sir. For drugs, it is a little complicated, but I can understand it, so it is not that complicated. One of my jobs is I serve as the chairman of the interdiction committee that works for the Office of National Drug Control Policy. We coordinate between DEA, Justice, Department of Defense, and others, we coordinate activities and share information. Part of it is a consolidated drug database.

We have a good idea on how much cocaine is produced in South America, we also have a good idea on how much is consumed on the streets of America, and we can judge that generally by how the price is going up, price is going down, and there are things that provide analysis to tell that.

There are about 800 metric tons produced in South America, there are about 400 tons that are consumed in the United States. On an average year, the Coast Guard interdicts, disrupts about 120 metric tons in the transit zone between South America into Central America. That is where you pick up the big loads.

The entire rest of the United States Federal, State, and local law enforcement agencies throughout millions of people interdict, seize about 40 metric tons countrywide, because they are in smaller loads when they come across, more difficult to find.

So that is why I feel so strongly about keeping our ships forward-deployed in the transit zones, so that we can interdict 4, 5, 6 metric tons at a time to keep them off the streets as they get here.

Plus, it is not just our streets. It is a destabilizing effect in Mexico and Central America that the transit of the drugs creates as well. Money and weapons going south to destabilize drugs coming north, it is a cycle that we have to break.

Mr. O'ROURKE. Thank you.

Thank you, Madam Chairwoman.

Mrs. MILLER. Thank you, Admiral.

Those numbers of how much is being consumed in the streets of America are really distressing. I have never heard that number before. That is mind-boggling.

At this time the Chairwoman now recognizes the gentlelady from Hawaii, Ms. Gabbard.

Ms. GABBARD. Thank you very much, Madam Chairwoman.

Sir, like my colleagues, I just want to say thank you so much for your commitment to service, your dedication to duty, and your leadership for Coasties everywhere.

Admiral PAPP. Thank you.

Ms. GABBARD. I had a chance to serve on my second deployment with some security forces in the Coast Guard who were based at the Kuwait naval base, and prior to that deployment, I had no idea that there were Coasties serving in the Middle East providing support to those missions, so I learned a lot from that perspective, as I have now in my interactions with the District 14 folks covering the Pacific, and just really appreciate all that the Coast Guard does.

In your written testimony, you specifically mentioned the renewed National focus on the Asia-Pacific region. Most people don't realize how large that space really is and the Coast Guard's central role in providing security there. Fourteenth District, as you know, is the Coast Guard's largest area of responsibility, covering 12.2 million square miles of land and sea. I am wondering if you can speak to what you see coming around the corner within this area, within the region, the Asia-Pacific region, from a threat perspective, what should we be anticipating from a homeland security viewpoint, and are we prepared from a resource perspective?

Admiral PAPP. I think in the Pacific-Asia region, the three things I see are drugs, migrants, and fisheries. Particularly our trust territories, let's go with fisheries, that 4.5 million-square-mile exclusive economic zone, a great deal of that is in the Pacific surrounding the Hawaiian islands, the trust territories, the islands, Guam, and others, and we do not have enough resources to keep a persistent presence to protect our fisheries. There are many incursions that are going on, and there are also partner countries out there that don't have much capacity as well.

We try to mitigate that. Actually the United States Navy has been very helpful. We have been putting law enforcement detachments on Navy ships that are transiting the area. Admiral Locklear has been very good in terms—and he has got a great relationship with our Coast Guard, in terms of putting a few extra days in for his Navy ships so that we can make passes through some of the areas out there where we want to protect our fishing and the migratory stocks that are out there.

So that has been a good program and helps us out, but I would clearly like to have more Coast Guard cutters out there and the time to be able to spend in those areas.

Those 800 metric tons of drugs, there is a big market in Australia right now, and I wouldn't be surprised if we start seeing— we have seen vessels being interdicted near Australia with multi-ton loads of cocaine.

Hawaii is not inconceivable. There could be drugs going into Hawaii as well. It is sort of a transit now back out across the Pacific that we are concerned about.

We have the precursors for methamphetamines that are produced in Asia that come across the Pacific generally going to south—to Central America for processing, but ultimately come across our borders, so we are working with partner nations to try and identify those cargoes before they get to our hemisphere.

Migrants: We are always concerned. Right now Australia, in fact, I consulted with Australia because they have such a huge illegal migration problem there, and they are looking at some of the practices that the United States Coast Guard uses in the Caribbean. It is a little bit different of a challenge for them. But we also look, there are oftentimes migrant vessels that will come across the North Pacific towards Canada or the West Coast of the United States that we have to be concerned about as well.

Ms. GABBARD. I have a brother who lives in Australia and was there towards the end of last year and had a chance to meet with the Australian Navy Fleet Commander, and he spoke very highly of the partnership and the lessons learned that they are gaining from our Coast Guard here.

You mentioned that you don't have enough cutters for District 14. I understand that District 14 is expected to get two National Security Cutters that will replace some of the aging cutters that have basically been extended beyond their designed service life. You know, I saw one of the cutters that was in dry dock at Pearl Harbor.

It is great that we have that asset there. But clearly when you get to that point the cost of continuing to refurbish these cutters beyond what they were designed for really doesn't make sense when it extends beyond the cost of bringing in a new cutter. I'm wondering when you expect these cutters to be put into service in Hawaii.

Admiral PAPP. The two National Security Cutters, we made that porting plan I think it was 2 years ago. I will get you the exact numbers for the record, but I think it is National Security Cutters Nos. 6 and 7 are going to Honolulu.

Given the production schedule, I would estimate that is probably going to be at least 4 or 5 years from now because No. 5 is under construction. I think they are starting on No. 6 and so it will be a couple years from now and we will keep a presence there, of course, until the new ships arrive if we have got enough room in the budget.

Ms. GABBARD. Thank you very much, sir. I appreciate it.

Mrs. MILLER. I thank the gentlelady very much.

I thank all the Members of the committee. If the committee Members, if anybody has additional questions, we will ask that the Commandant would respond to those in writing, if they ask. Pursuant to Committee Rule 7(e), the hearing record will be held—yes, Ranking Member.

Ms. JACKSON LEE. First of all, let me indicate that I have a Cabinet officer that I had to speak to in just a moment.

But I want to thank the Commandant and I wanted to make sure that in his response would he share with me my answer to the questions on the TWIC card.

Admiral PAPP. Yes, ma'am.

Ms. JACKSON LEE. I appreciate very much.

I know there were a lot of questions, so I am very interested in that and very interested in your counsel on how we can make that more efficient and more effective.

I think in particular, if I may, Madam Chairwoman, just read this question too: Should this Government-centric premise to the TWIC card be revisited? That was based upon using this approach to port security credentialing in which DHS is responsible for enrollment, card issuance, and security vetting for TWIC; is that the best option?

Then, what needs to be done to ensure the TWIC program delivers the security benefits Congress envisioned while not unduly burdening workers or disrupting our ports? Also you might comment on the Coast Guard role.

I thank you for that.

Admiral PAPP. Yes, ma'am.

Ms. JACKSON LEE. Thank you very much. Thank you, Madam Chairwoman.

Mrs. MILLER. Certainly. I thank the gentlelady for those questions.

Again I am sure the Commandant will respond to those to the committee and will get the answers to you.

Pursuant to the Committee Rule 7(e), the hearing record will be held open for 10 days.

Again, Admiral, we just want to thank you so sincerely for your many, many years of service to the Nation and look forward to working with you in the future as well.

Good luck to your wife. I didn't realize she was going to be the sponsor of the *Hamilton*. That is terrific. We appreciate it. You have been a great advocate for the Coast Guard, and I think as you can see from this committee Coast Guard had some very, very deep wells of goodwill toward the Coast Guard and the men and women in the service and what they do for our Nation.

We thank you very much.

Admiral PAPP. Thank you, ma'am. It has been an honor.

Mrs. MILLER. With that, without objection, the committee stands adjourned.

[Whereupon, at 11:08 a.m., the subcommittee was adjourned.]

APPENDIX

QUESTIONS FROM HONORABLE STEVEN M. PALAZZO FOR ROBERT J. PAPP

Question 1. What is the strategy for modernizing and recapitalizing the USCG air fleet while minimizing the impact on the USCG budget, and how does the Avionics 1 Upgrade (A1U) upgrade program fit into that strategy?

Answer. Response was not received at the time of publication.

Question 2. How does the USCG plan to cover a multi-year operational gap from the time the HC–130Hs are transferred to the USFS to the time the first fully-missionized C27J reaches initial operational capability?

Answer. Response was not received at the time of publication.

Question 3. When will the USCG implement the next phase of A1U upgrades to the HC–130H airframes?

Answer. Response was not received at the time of publication.

Question 4. What is the acquisition plan for the HC–130J?

Answer. Response was not received at the time of publication.

Question 5. How would any future acquisition of any additional HC–130 J models impact the acquisition of additional National Security Cutters in the fleet?

Answer. Response was not received at the time of publication.

Question 6. In 2013, the Commandant testified that the Avionics 1 Upgrade (A1U) installations on HC–130H aircraft enhanced the capability of the HC–130H fleet by replacing aging/obsolete equipment, and updating avionics to comply with Communications Navigation Surveillance/Air Traffic Management (CNS/ATM).[1] Considering the length of time (an estimated 4 years) for the C27J to be fully mission-ready, is the A1U program still front-and-center of your near-term air asset recapitalization plan?

Answer. Response was not received at the time of publication.

Question 7. Is acquiring HC–130Js in the next 5 to 10 years economically feasible in light of the demands on the USCG budget for surface assets such as the National Security Cutter, Fast Response Cutter, Offshore Patrol Cutter, and Polar Icebreaker?

Answer. Response was not received at the time of publication.

Question 8. Further considering that the A1U program is a key part of the USCGs plan to "Build Essential Coast Guard Capability for the Nation", does the USCG plan to now, or in the near future cancel or reduce the A1U program?[2]

Answer. Response was not received at the time of publication.

Question 9. How can Mississippi support the mission of the USCG air fleet?

Answer. Response was not received at the time of publication.

○

---

[1] Written testimony of U.S. Coast Guard Commandant Admiral Robert Papp, Jr. for a House Committee on Transportation and Infrastructure, Subcommittee on Coast Guard and Maritime Transportation hearing titled "The President's Fiscal Year 2014 Budget Request for Coast Guard and Maritime Transportation Programs" Release Date: April 16, 2013. 2167 Rayburn House Office Building.

[2] U.S. Coast Guard Fact Sheet—Fiscal Year 2014 President's Budget. April 10, 2013.